W9-CFG-652

LIBRARY
FULMAR ROAD SCHOOL
MAHOPAC, N.Y. 10541

811
Tur
F20933

MANY VOICES
ONE SONG

Songs of Our Ancestors

Poems about Native Americans

By Mark Turcotte

Illustrated by Kathleen S. Presnell

CHILDRENS PRESS®
CHICAGO

I'd like to thank Kathleen for her beautiful artwork, Alice Flanagan for her editorial help and patience, and Carlos Cumpián for his support and encouragement. -- M.T.

Humble thanks to my dear, supportive family. Special gratitude to Mary Heleniak for her confidence and guidance in those formative years. -- K.S.P.

We'd like to dedicate this book to our great-niece, Quaila Marie!

Library of Congress Cataloging--in--Publication Data

Turcotte, Mark.
     Songs of our ancestors: poems about native Americans / by Mark
Turcotte; illustrated by Kathleen S. Presnell.
          p. cm.-- (Many voices, one song)
     Summary: A collection of more than twenty poems that focus on
famous North American Indians and events in their history.
     ISBN 0-516-05154-7
 I. Indians of North America--Biography--Juvenile poetry.
 2. Indians of North America--History--Juvenile poetry.
 3. Childrens' poetry, American. [1. Indians of North America-Poetry.
 2. American poetry.] I. Presnell, Kathleen S., ill.
 II. Title. III. Series.
 PS3570.U627S66 1995
 8II'.54--dc20   94-38380
                                                          CIP
                                                          AC

Copyright ©1995 Childrens Press®,Inc.
All rights reserved.
Published simultaneously in Canada.
Printed in the United States of America.
1 2 3 4 5 6 7 8 9 0 R 00 01 02 03 04 99 98 97 96 95

Project Editor: Alice Flanagan
Design and Electronic Production:
   PCI Design Group, San Antonio, Texas
Engraver: Liberty Photoengravers
Printer: Lake Book Manufacturing, Inc.

Introduction

With this book of poem-songs, I hope to share with you a very old Native American tradition – a tradition of teaching and learning our history through storytelling. Some of the stories in this book are happy, and some of them are sad. What is important is that they are OUR stories. I am honored to share them with you and hope that they will help you discover what you didn't know before. You might even see yourself in the stories; or maybe they will inspire you to tell a story about your ancestors that I will be able to read someday. After all, we all have stories to tell.

Please find others who will sit together with you in a circle and read the stories. And as you read, listen – to the *Songs of Our Ancestors*.

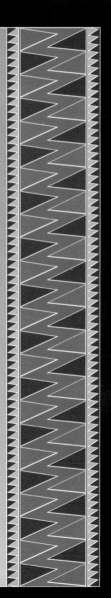

Table of Contents

Songs of Our Ancestors

In the snow that falls upon the mountain tops,
in the wind that howls across the plains,
we hear the songs of our ancestors.
In a glint of Sun upon a meadow thick with flowers,
in the rumble of the clouds that hold the summer rains,
we hear the songs of our ancestors.

In the laughter of the children,
in the wisdom of an Elder's eyes,
in coyote calls across the desert,
in the wings of hawks against the sky.

From forest to farm to factory,
through the cities and the slums,
within the powwow circle,
in the beating of our drums.

The songs they sing fill up our dreams,
the music reminds us of who we are.
Their ancient voices give us courage
to bravely reach for any star.

For the more we strive and struggle
to be the best that we can be,
we honor those who came before us,
and their songs shape our destiny.

Long before there was a United States,
in the time of the Thirteen Colonies,
there was a union created
between six Indian nations,
known as the Iroquois Confederacy.

By 1735, these unfriendly Indian nations
had joined together as one.
In the interest of peace and security,
they pledged cooperation and unity,
forever under the sun.

They lived in the land now known as New York State,
the Tuscarora, Mohawk, and Onondaga,
and the Longhouse was the symbol of their union
with the Seneca, Oneida, and Cayuga.

On wampum belts they recorded
their Great Law of Peace,
which stated that leaders
must be servants of the people,
and everyone had freedom of speech.

The Great Law also provided
protection from repression,
rights for women,
laws to be amended,
and freedom of religious expression.

Some say that the U.S. Constitution
was based upon the Great Law of Peace,
that the Longhouse was the model
for a perfect union,
that would survive and never cease.

# The Seminole

Here's the story of a "runaway people,"
the story of the Seminole,
who settled in the southeastern United States
when it was under Spanish control.

A mix of people from many tribes,
who had fled from war and strife,
were joined by many African slaves,
who had escaped from plantation life.

Against encroachment of white settlers,
the Seminoles' bond was strong.
They sucessfully kept out slave catchers
but were unable to do so for long.

A campaign to drive out the Seminole
led to destruction, treachery, and hate.
In 1817, the first Seminole War took place,
and in 1819, Spain ceded Florida
to the United States.

Under Osceola's expert leadership,
the Seminole were determined to stay.
Each time soldiers came to remove them,
they were quickly driven away.

After the second Seminole War of 1842,
a truce came and there was talk of peace,
but when Osceola arrived to negotiate,
he was captured and never released.

That treacherous act brought an end to the wars
and to any opportunity for the Seminole to stay,
though some managed to hide in the Florida swamps,
where their descendants are living today.

Suwanee River

St. John's River

ST. AUGUSTINE

FLORIDA

Indian River

Lake
Kissimmee

Kissimmee River

TAMPA BAY

Peace River

LAKE
OKEECHOBEE

GULF OF
MEXICO

THE
EVERGLADE

Area Assigned to the Seminoles - 1839

Atlantic Ocean

11

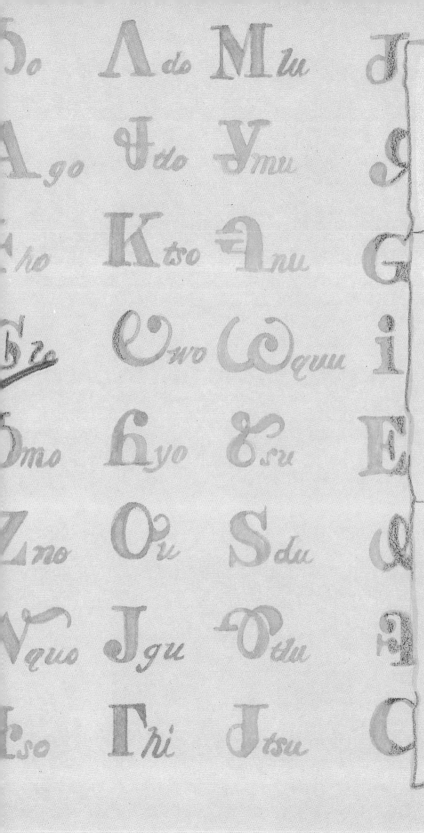

Sequoyah

Sequoyah was a solitary child,
who loved to think and to work with his hands,
with rare patience and concentration,
that served him well as he grew to be a man.

He was intrigued by the white man's language,
with the way it could be written and read,
how by drawing on a piece of paper,
one could understand the words that another said.

Over many years he created symbols
for his peoples' words and sounds.
In 1821, he finished his task,
and Cherokee words could be read and written down.

In time, Sequoyah's system of writing
unified and strengthened the Cherokee.
They could communicate across distance and time.
His enduring gift made history.

Sequoyah, silversmith and painter,
born in the mountains of eastern Tennessee,
left a legacy of love to his people,
an alphabet for the great Cherokee.

The Trail of Tears

President Andrew Jackson,
elected in 1828,
believed in westward expansion
of what was then the United States.

The U.S. policy was to claim every inch of land,
as far as the eye could see.
Every tree and rock and grain of sand,
they would take to meet their greed.

"Get rid of the Indians," the pioneers cried,
"We want the land as our own.
Why, they're not even civilized.
They don't really want a home."

"We'll make a new law," said Jackson,
"one to clear Indians out of the way.
I'll send soldiers to force quick action
and to take them someplace else to stay."

So the Indian Removal Act was signed,
authorizing relocation that took years.
The Cherokee were forced to leave their lives behind,
marched, and died on the Trail of Tears.

The Cherokee were left, like many others,
with few blankets, supplies, or winter clothes.
Sons and daughters, fathers and mothers,
thousands were swept away in the bitter snows.

This is one more story of greed and shame,
one more injustice caused by hate and fear,
one more tradgedy that was given a name,
the terrible Trail of Tears.

ILLINOIS

KANSAS

MISSOURI

Springfield

Tahlequah

OKLAHOMA

ARKANSAS

MISSISSIPPI

INDIANA

KENTUCKY

Nashville

TENNESSEE

NORTH
CAROLINA

ALABAMA   GEORGIA

15

Geronimo

SAN CARLOS
RESERVATION

SAN
CARLOS
AGENCY

GILA RIVER

TUCSON

TOMBSTONE

UNITED STATES

SONORA

N

When the Apache were forced
by the U.S. Army
to San Carlos Reservation,
one man stood tall
and refused to go,
shocking the American nation.

"I was not born for farming,"
said bold Geronimo.
"I won't build fences,
and I won't plow fields.
It's not the life I know."

Geronimo led his Chiricahua band
into the canyons and the hills.
That's where the army lost them,
even though they had good tracking skills.

For ten long years
the army chased him
in circles here and there.
"How can this be,"
the worn-out soldiers cried,
"he's vanished into thin air!"

Some cursed his name,
yet many cheered.
His legend grew and grew.
He was admired
and won respect
for what he tried to do.

Then General Miles,
with five thousand men,
surrounded Geronimo,
who was forced to surrender
and was taken in chains
from the freedom he had known.

From that September day in 1886,
he was considered a prisoner of war,
held in Florida and Alabama,
then finally in Oklahoma,
never to return to the land he'd fought for.

Although he's gone,
his name lives on
in memories of long ago,
in the hearts of those
who admire his courage
and shout, "Geronimo!"

NEW MEXICO

WARM
SPRINGS

RIO GRANDE

MIMBRES RIVER

SILVER CITY

GILA TRAIL

MEXICO

JANOS

CHIHUAHUA

Crazy Horse

He was born among the brave Lakota,
beside the sacred hills of black.
To this day they speak of him,
while some pray he will come back.

He was given his name in a mystical dream
of a warrior on a wild horse.
He wore a streak of lightning on his face,
and spirits guided his life's course.

A boy of courage, who grew up strong,
learning to be a true Lakota man,
living in harmony and dignity,
respectful of the giving land.

Until settlers and miners came
with plows and picks to wound the Earth,
with guns to kill the buffalo,
to steal the hills that gave him birth.

Then Crazy Horse, his heart on fire,
rode to war against the whites,
fighting to save Lakota ways
and the land that was their life.

He resisted the invasion of railroad men,
prospectors, and the cavalry.
Against General Custer at the Little Bighorn,
his warriors thundered to victory.

But enemies far outnumbered the Lakota.
Game was scarce and winter was on its way.
Crazy Horse gave up the fight for his people,
brought them to the Red Cloud Agency to stay.

In 1877, on that Nebraska reservation,
Crazy Horse regretted that he'd quit.
Facing imprisonment, he resisted one more time
and was killed by a soldier's bayonet.

Yes, he was born among the brave Lakota,
beside the sacred hills of black,
and to this day they speak of him,
while some pray he will come back.

The Lakota share a mystic vision
guiding their life's course,
of a warrior with lightning on his face,
just like the man called Crazy Horse.

Crazy
Horse
Attack

Cheyenne
Camp

Sioux
Camp

N

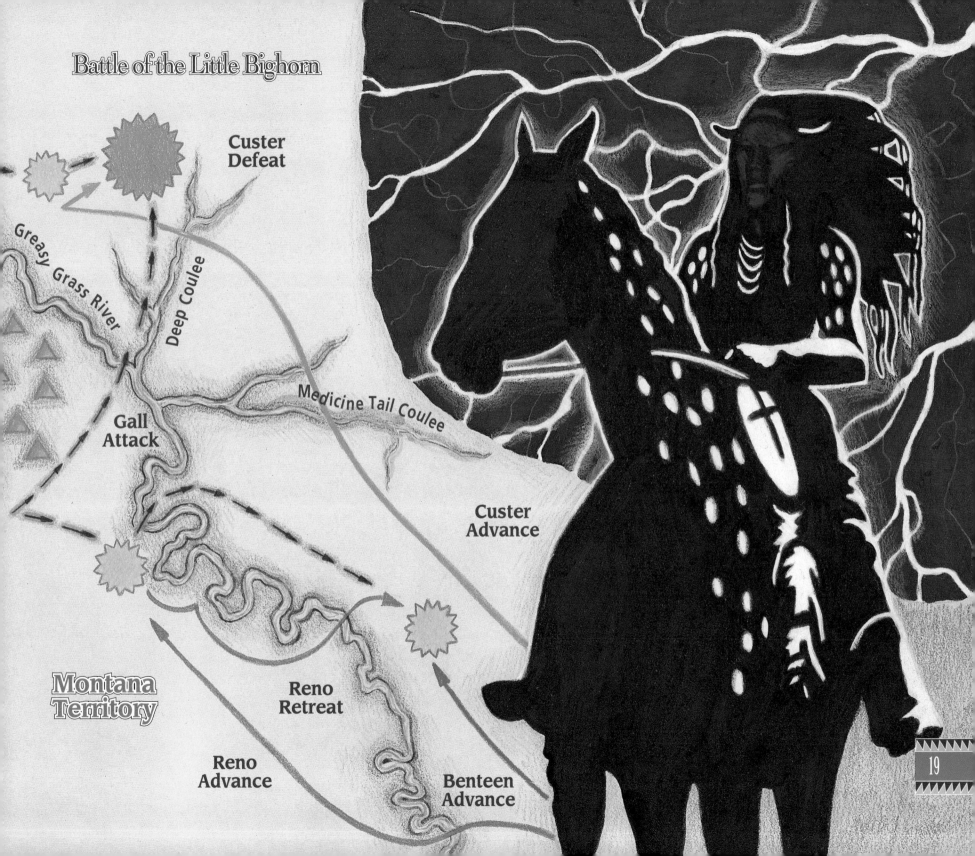

Battle of the Little Bighorn

Custer
Defeat

Greasy Grass River

Deep Coulee

Medicine Tail Coulee

Gall
Attack

Custer
Advance

Montana
Territory

Reno
Retreat

Reno
Advance

Benteen
Advance

19

Sitting Bull

At ten he killed his first buffalo,
at fourteen he counted coup,
soon after, in his vision quest,
his tested heart proved true.

Sitting Bull, Teton Lakota,
respected chief and spiritual man,
clever politician and diplomat,
of the great Hunkpapa band.

Far and wide across the rolling prairies,
the Lakota were free to roam,
until the day U.S. soldiers came
with treaties that forced them from their home.

When a giant wave of settlers followed,
Sitting Bull fought against the tide,
not signing the Fort Laramie Treaty,
which he knew was a shameless lie.

Settlers proved Sitting Bull was right
when they took the Black Hills for their own,
though the treaty said the Hills were sacred
and should forever be left alone.

Sitting Bull, with many other chiefs,
went to war to protect the land.
They won the Battle of the Little Bighorn
that pushed Custer to his last stand.

But in their hearts they all knew
that the end of Lakota ways was near.
Sitting Bull surrendered to the army
who kept him a prisoner two years.

He lived at Standing Rock Reservation,
for a time, he joined a Wild West show.
He was closely watched by the government,
because his following continued to grow.

The army sent Indian Bureau police
to arrest him and bring him in.
In the confusion, shots were fired,
and Sitting Bull lay dead in the end.

Without Sitting Bull as a symbol of strength,
the Plains Indians soon gave up their fight.
They felt lost and alone in the white world
without Sitting Bull's wise, guiding light.

WOUNDED KNEE

It was in the harsh winter of 1890,
on the Standing Rock Reservation,
that Sitting Bull's band faced hardship,
disease, and the certainty of starvation.

Many sought safety in Big Foot's band
at their camp near Wounded Knee Creek.
Most were women and children,
most were old, sick, and weak.

In was in that cruel winter of 1890,
that the cavalry captured Big Foot's band.
Surrounded by guns, Big Foot surrendered,
knowing it was useless to make a stand.

In the morning, as the camp was searched,
suddenly the soldiers' guns began to blaze.
More than two hundred Lakotas were killed,
while many lay wounded in the cold, smoky haze.

It was in the bloody winter of 1890,
that people heard of the massacre by name,
that Indian resistance and hopes for survival
ended in tragedy and national shame.

Wovoka

By the end of the 1800s,
little was left of the Indian Nations.
Those who weren't killed by soldiers or disease
were forced to live on wretched reservations.

With little hope in their hearts and less food in their bellies,
they turned to Wovoka, a Paiute holy man,
who preached that soon the buffalo would return
and Indian ancestors would return to the land.

"Reject the ways of the whites," he said,
and he taught them new prayers and chants.
The people gathered all across the plains
to bring back the old ways through the Ghost Dance.

When the government became alarmed by the Ghost Dance
and the movement that Wovoka had begun,
they sent out soldiers to put an end to the new belief
and to arrest all the leaders one by one.

On December 15, 1890, Sitting Bull was murdered.
On the 29th, Big Foot was cut down at Wounded Knee.
Then the people lost faith in the teachings of Wovoka,
and the Ghost Dance faded into obscurity.

Chief Joseph

Joseph was a peaceful Chief
of a Nez Perce band,
living in the lands of Oregon and Idaho,
in the green Wallowa Valley
where they hunted game
and fished for salmon since so long ago.

For years the Nez Perce
had traded with trappers
and had friendly relations with whites,
but when gold was discovered
and treaties were broken,
Nez Perce warriors began to fight.

Chief Joseph urged calm,
but warriors fought settlers,
and then army troops arrived.
Outnumbered in size,
the Nez Perce knew
there was only one way they'd survive.

With all hope of living in the valley gone,
they fled east and then north
for the country of the great buffalo.
The trail was rough
for the young and the old,
in the mountains the going was slow.

Trailing them, and not far behind,
rode General Howard
with soldiers, cannons, and guns.
Guided by Chief Joseph
and his military chiefs,
the Nez Perce fought on the run.

For four long months
they outwitted the army
as they neared the Canadian border.
But, pinned down by Howard,
thirty miles from freedom,
Chief Joseph gave his last order.

Exhaustion and bad weather,
and lack of food had stopped them.
Many of their chiefs were dead.
On October 5, 1877, Joseph surrendered.
"From where the sun now stands,
I will fight no more forever," he said.

After their surrender,
the Nez Perce were promised
a reservation near their old land.
But that promise was forgotten,
like so many others,
and Chief Joseph was left, a broken man.

Washington

Nez
Perce
Route

Oregon

Bitterro
Mtns.

Salmon Riv

Idaho

Snake River

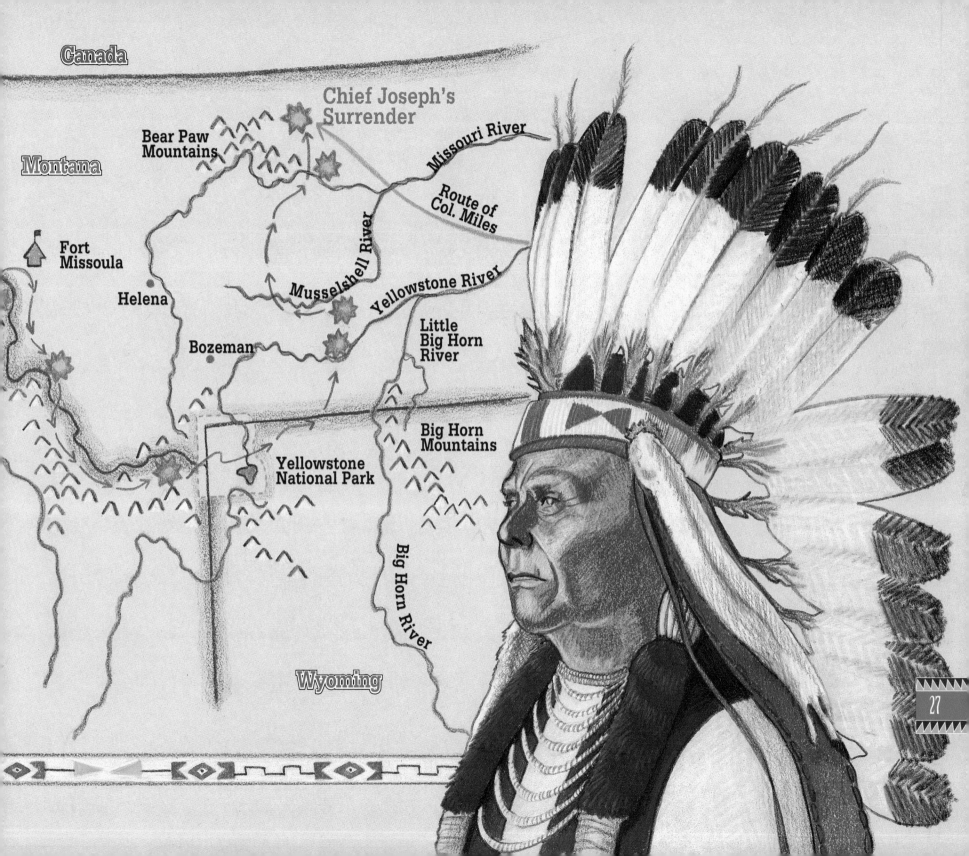

Canada

Chief Joseph's
Surrender

Bear Paw
Mountains

Montana

Missouri River

Route of
Col. Miles

Fort
Missoula

Musselshell River

Yellowstone River

Helena

Little
Big Horn
River

Bozeman

Big Horn
Mountains

Yellowstone
National Park

Big Horn River

Wyoming

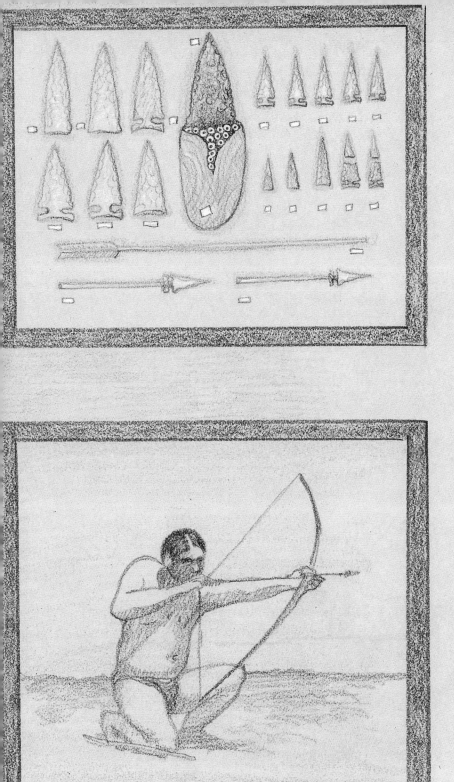

Ishi

Of all the Yahi people,
Ishi was the last,
when he walked out of the California hills,
like a shadow from the past.

He was a lonely survivor
of a small northern band,
one of four that made the Yana Nation,
that once thrived on the rocky land.

An anthropologist, Thomas Waterman,
heard about this Yahi man.
He came to his rescue,
extending a friendly hand.

Ishi was invited to San Francisco,
to live at the university museum,
where he taught Waterman about his Yahi life,
and where people came for miles just to see him.

He taught them Yahi skills,
how to make tools from wood and stone,
how to hunt and gather food
when you're in the wilderness, alone.

What Ishi shared for four and a half years
can never be bought or measured.
When he died on March 25, 1916,
He left knowledge that will always be treasured.

WILL ROGERS

They called him the Cherokee Cowboy,
because he could rope and ride.
Will Rogers, from Oklahoma,
was famous far and wide.

From the Wild West shows to the Ziegfield Follies,
everyone laughed at his jokes,
and with his lariat tricks and down-home humor,
he won the hearts of regular folks.

He made wisecracks about the U.S. Congress
and events in the daily news,
always twirling a rope with a grin on his face,
in his chaps and cowboy shoes.

Ask your Great-Grandma if she's heard of him,
go ask your Great-Grandpa, too;
ask if they recall the Cherokee Cowboy,
and I'll bet you that they do.

Jim Thorpe

Go Jim Thorpe!
baseball star,
run like the wind across the field,
to three major league teams
and plenty of hits,
run like the wind across the field.

Go Jim Thorpe!
football star,
pass like an arrow across the field,
to the All-America team
and undefeated seasons,
pass like an arrow across the field.

Go Jim Thorpe!
Olympic star,
leap like a deer across the field,
to new world records
and two gold medals,
leap like a deer across the field.

Go Jim Thorpe!
Native American star,
we sing your story out loud.
You're like the wind,
true as an arrow,
swift as a deer,
you made your people proud.

Code Talkers of World War Two

They never gave the enemy
any clues,
the Indian code talkers
of World War Two.

They spoke their native languages
on the radio –
the Choctaw, Comanche,
and the Navajo.

In special units
of the proud Marines,
they were heroes
behind the scenes.

American secrets
were never found
because of Indian code talkers
and their Native sound.

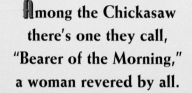

Te Ata

Among the Chickasaw
there's one they call,
"Bearer of the Morning,"
a woman revered by all.

Te Ata, the storyteller,
exemplifies Native pride.
Through the power of her words,
ancestors and traditions will survive.

Once honored by Eleanor Roosevelt,
who gave to a lake Te Ata's name,
honored by the people of Oklahoma,
who placed her in their Hall of Fame,

Te Ata, dramatic storyteller,
epitomizes Native pride
through the power of her voice,
keeping tradition alive.

Buffy Sainte-Marie

A shy little girl
in her daydream world,
who loved to write poetry,
became a star
when she played guitar,
singer Buffy Sainte-Marie.

Her songs about Cree
and how life should be
brought attention to her name.
Her songs about poverty,
exposing inequality,
added to her fame.

Protesting war,
violence, and more
Buffy still sings today.
No longer a shy little girl
in a daydream world,
she has important things to say.

A.I.M.

American Indian Movement

Red Power!
Red Power!
Was the cry across the land.
Red Power!
Red Power!
It was time to take a stand.

Red Power!
Red Power!
Unity, side by side.
Red Power!
Red Power!
A call for Native pride.

In the 1970s,
from the four directions
committed people came.
They raised their voices,
marched together as one,
beneath the flag of AIM.

Maria Tallchief

An Osage from Oklahoma,
dancer full of grace,
swift and strong,
lean and long,
and very fair of face.

An Osage from Oklahoma,
leaping to the clouds,
elegant, flawless prima,
New York City ballerina,
pleasing all the crowds.

WILL SAMPSON

Big Will Sampson, a proud Muscogee,
stood six-foot-seven head to toe,
a construction worker and oil field hand,
and a brave bull rider in the rodeo.

Then he got a break in a Hollywood movie,
One Flew Over the Cuckoo's Nest,
and everyone agreed he'd found his calling,
his acting was a great success.

He fought for better roles for Native actors,
who were struggling for opportunities and rights.
He spoke out against prejudice and bigotry,
brought awareness of Indian issues to a new height.

Big Will Sampson, a proud Muscogee,
was someone Native Americans were proud to know.
This artist and actor, with the heart of a giant,
stood six-foot-seven head to toe.

Wilma Mankiller

From a poor family of farmers,
Wilma Mankiller grew up to be
the principal chief and leader
of the Nation of Cherokee.

It was once part of their tradition
for women to share power with men.
Ancestry was traced through the mother's clan,
important decisions were made by them.

Yet, there were many who doubted
that Wilma could ever succeed.
It was these she soon won over
with her accomplishments and deeds.

Working tirelessly night and day
to end years of poverty,
she implemented several plans
to improve the Cherokee economy.

Wilma Mankiller, first woman chief,
of the Nation of Cherokee,
governs well in difficult times,
a leader to admire for you and me.

LOUISE ERDRICH

Her passion for words
came at an early age,
when with pen in hand
she first wrote a story on a page.

Then her passion for words,
like a flame grew brighter,
and ever since that day,
she knew she'd be a writer.

Louise Erdrich, an Ojibwa,
has served her people well,
creating in her novels
tales that no one else could tell.

With stories about families
across the generations,
she takes her readers on a ride
of intrigue and fascination.

Her passion for words
has brought critical acclaim,
numerous awards,
and best-sellers to her name.

She's an author of distinction,
with a passion for all things,
and we not only read her books,
we listen to them sing!

Glossary

accomplishment Something completed successfully.

amend Change, as a law.

ancestry Family history.

anthropologist (an thru PAWL u jist) A scientist who studies human beings: where they live, how they live there, how they behave, and so forth.

authorize Give permission for or approve of.

bigotry Beliefs and actions based on hatred for a group or groups.

cavalry Soldiers who fight on horseback.

cede (seed) Surrender or give up, especially land.

chaps Leather coverings worn over trousers by horseback riders (such as ranch hands).

Chiricahua (chir u KAQ wu) A band of the Apache people of Arizona.

clan A group of people, usually related and/or sharing certain interests.

committed Serious about doing something; dedicated.

count coup (koo) A sioux (soo) test of skill in which a warrior would count each touch of an enemy (the coup) as proof of his bravery.

critical acclaim Praise from critics, the people who normally judge creative work, such as writing or art.

Custer, George Armstrong (1839-1876) American cavalry commander and Indian fighter. Died in battle (known as Custer's Last Stand) with warriors led by Crazy Horse at Little Bighorn (Montana).

descendant (di SEN dunt) A person's child, grandchild, great-grandchild, and so forth.

destiny Future.

dignity Pride and self-respect that shows in the way a person behaves.

diplomat A person who represents his or her nation in its dealings with other countries. Also, someone who is skillful in handling such affairs.

distinction Importance, excellence.

economy Activities that relate to business and industry, including jobs and wages.

encroachment (in CROCH munt) The moving in and taking over of something, such as land.

enduring Lasting.

epitomize (i PI tu myz) Stand as an example of.

exemplify (ig ZEM plu fy) Stand for; be a model of.

expose Make known to the public; reveal faults or crimes.

flawless Perfect, free of mistakes.

generation All the members of a family who grow up at about the same time.

"Geronimo" A cry used by paratroopers as they jump from a plane.

Ghost Dance A group dance among Native Americans that was believed would help return the dead and their traditional ways of life.

harsh Very hard, difficult.

implement Carry out, put into effect.

inequality (i ni KWAW lu tee) Conditions that are not equal for all people or groups of people.

injustice A wrong; an unfair action.

intrigue (IN treeg) Secret plans and schemes.

intrigued (in TREEG'D) Interested.

Iroquois Confederacy (IR u kwoi) A grouping of five tribes (Mohawk, Oneida, Onondaga, Cayuga, and Seneca) founded in 1570. Joined by the Tuscarora in 1722.

lariat (LA ree ut) Lasso; rope with adjustable loop on the end.

legacy (LE gu see) Gift from those who have lived before to those who come after them.

Longhouse Typical long building in which Iroquois families lived together; also symbol of the Iroquois Confederacy.

mystic vision Dream in which events seem to have special, often religious, meaning.

mystical Having a special meaning; not explainable in ordinary ways.

negotiate Speak with others in order to come to an agreement on a subject on which the sides hold different opinions.

numerous (NOO mu rus) Many.

obscurity (ob SKYOOR u tee) State of being unknown, unimportant, or forgotten.

Paiute (PY yoot) Of an American Indian people originally of Utah, Arizona, Nevada, and California.

passion Strong liking, love.

politician A person who serves in government as an elected or appointed official.

prima (PREE mu) Prima, or leading, ballerina in a ballet company.

principal First; most important.

prospector Anyone searching an area for gold or other valuable materials.

repression Being kept down or held back.

revered Beloved, respected.

sacred Holy; intended for religious use.

security Safety.

spiritual Concerned with religious matters.

strife Fighting, quarreling.

thrive Do well.

treacherous (TRECH u rus) False.

treachery (TRECH u ree) An action that reveals broken promises or lies and may put the lives of those who believed them in danger.

treaty An agreement, usually between nations.

unify (YOO ni fy) Bring together.

vision quest A Native American rite in which adolescents fast and dream. The dream reveals the young person's guardian spirit.

wampum belt Beads made of polished shells, strung together.

wretched (RE chud) Miserable, unpleasant.

Zigfield Follies A yearly theater production from 1907 - 1927, put on by Florenz Ziegfield.

About the Author and the Illustrator

Mark Turcotte and Kathleen S. Presnell are married and living in Chicago with their son, Ezra Cole. They share their home with three cats and one very large dog. Their dream is to one day live deep in the woods near big water.

Mark is an Ojibway who spent part of his childhood on North Dakota's Turtle Mountain Reservation. Later, he grew up in and around Potterville, Michigan. Before moving to Chicago two years ago, he lived and worked in several locations throughout the United States. He has always loved writing and now enjoys performing his work, as well. Mark is also the author of *The Feathered Heart*, a book of poems for grownups, published by MARCH/Abrazo.

Kathleen graduated with a Bachelor of Fine Arts degree from the Minneapolis College of Art and Design. Most recently, she collaborated with her husband, illustrating another book of poetry. In her spare time, she designs product for the gift and housewares industry. Kathleen has been drawing forever and plans to continue.

© Steve Greiner.

F20933

811
TUR
Turcotte, Mark

Songs of our
ancestors

$21.30

DATE			

LIBRARY
FULMAR ROAD SCHOOL
MAHOPAC, N.Y. 10541

FULMAR ROAD ELEM SCH/LIBY
FULMAR ROAD
MAHOPAC NY
                        10541
04/06/1996

000813   9109976 B

BAKER & TAYLOR